Kevin Crossley-Holland has translate
(Penguin Classics). His last two collectior.
Yes (1996) and *Poems from East Anglia* (.
Enitharmon, and he is also a Carnegie M   ...unor for
children. He is now working on a cycle of p.   ... about the mysterious
Moored Man, and a three-part novel for children that embodies
retellings of the Arthurian legends.

Simon Drew has illustrated fourteen books of his own nonsense verse
and puns, and has recently completed a set of satirical postcards for the
National Portrait Gallery. His Dartmouth Gallery has been open for
eighteen years.

Lawrence Sail has edited several anthologies, including *First and Always:
poems for Great Ormond Street Hospital* (Faber, 1988). His two most
recent collections of poems are *Out of Land: New and Selected Poems*
(1992) and *Building into Air* (1995), both published by Bloodaxe Books.
He lives in Exeter.

THE NEW EXETER BOOK
OF RIDDLES

Edited by Kevin Crossley-Holland and Lawrence Sail

with drawings by Simon Drew

London
ENITHARMON PRESS
1999

First published in 1999
by the Enitharmon Press
36 St George's Avenue
London N7 0HD

Reprinted, 1999

Distributed in Europe
by Littlehampton Book Services
through Signature Book Representation
2 Little Peter Street
Manchester M15 4PS

Distributed in the USA and Canada
by Dufour Editions Inc.
PO Box 7, Chester Springs
PA 19425, USA

British Library Cataloguing-in-Publication Data.
A catalogue record for this book is available
from the British Library.

The Enitharmon Press gratefully acknowledges
the support of Exeter Phoenix
in the production of this book.

Set in 10pt Bembo by Bryan Williamson, Frome,
and printed in Great Britain by
The Cromwell Press, Wiltshire

HEN IN LADLE

For Helen and Linda

One keen, and leggy as a heron,
One spring-heeled, a bubbling lark:
Both in the swim, challenging those poets
Who nibble with their feet at the watermark.

ELK IN WREN CAVE

Acknowledgements

The publisher and editors would like to thank Nick Ewbank and Andy Morley, the Director and the Arts Manager of Exeter Phoenix, for their assistance in the preparation of this book.

Acknowledgement is also due to the publications listed below, in which the riddles (or versions of them) by the following writers have appeared:

Jane Beeson, *Quartz* (Headland, 1997); Tilla Brading, *Shearsman*; Gillian Clarke, *E*; Elizabeth Garrett, *The Rule of Three* (Bloodaxe, 1991); Mimi Khalvati, *Entries on Light* (Carcanet, 1997); Roger McGough, *Nailing the Shadow* (Penguin, 1987); Paul Muldoon, *Hay* (Faber, 1998); Carol Rumens, *Holding Pattern* (Blackstaff, 1998).

Selima Hill's riddle is one of a series commissioned by The National Museum of Science and Technology.

Contents

Foreword

The Riddles

Answers

Foreword

There are good reasons for the popularity of the riddle. It is the most adaptable of forms, a shape-changer that is at one moment a tricksy one-liner loved by young children, and at the next an extended and sophisticated metaphor. Its subject is each and any element of creation, animate and inanimate; or, on occasion, creation itself. Because the subjects of riddles are more often material than abstract – describing artefacts and the natural world surrounding us – they tend to bridge generations. And the tone of the riddle: it is typically teasing, sometimes shocking, sometimes bawdy, ruminative, mysterious, elegiac.

Wittgenstein asserted that 'The riddle does not exist. If a question can be framed at all, it is also possible to answer it.' But despite this awkward proposition, the form has in fact long prospered in both folk and literary guises. The earliest surviving riddles are Babylonian and almost three thousand years old; incised on wax tablets, they describe a shuttle in a loom, and rain-clouds. There are riddles in the Rig Veda, the Bible and the Koran. And there is the celebrated riddle which the Sphinx, that terrifying creature with the head of a woman, the body and tail of a lion, and the wings of a bird, put to the Bœotians: 'What is it that has one voice, and goes on four legs in the morning, two legs at noon and three legs in the evening?'

Ask that of a class of primary or elementary schoolchildren and the likelihood is that, like Oedipus, one of them will begin to work things out and perhaps fathom an answer.

★

When Leofric, the first bishop of Exeter, died in 1072, he bequeathed to the cathedral library *.i. mycel englisc boc be gehwilcum þingum on leoðwisan geworht*: one large book in English verse about various subjects. This manuscript, one of only four surviving miscellanies of Anglo-Saxon poetry, contains not only magnificent Germanic, Christian and elegiac poems but ninety-six riddles (originally, there were one hundred, but one folio of the manuscript is missing). Some of these delightful riddles elaborate on subjects in three earlier Latin collections, and some of them are original. They describe natural phenomena, animal and bird life, weaponry, domestic objects, and objects associated with Christian worship (a church bell, a chalice, a bible), music and writing. A few of the Anglo-Saxon riddles use runes but the great majority are metaphorical.

Aristotle was the first to say something about the ground shared by riddle and metaphor, in his *Rhetoric*:

> While metaphor is a very frequent instrument of clever sayings, another or additional instrument is deception, as people are more clearly conscious of having learned something from their sense of surprise at the way in which the sentence ends and their soul seems to say, 'Quite true and I had missed the point.' This, too, is the result of pleasure afforded by clever riddles; they are instructive and metaphorical in their expression.

There is something else to add about the metaphorical riddle. It connects. To say that an apple is not only round and red or green but that it weeps when you bite it; that it is speckled and freckled; that it is a sphere, and contains dark secrets: all this suggests and establishes relationships between the apple and a number of other subjects. In this way, a riddle may not only be pleasurable but also have a healing power.

★

It is the Anglo-Saxon Exeter Book riddles which have occasioned and given shape to *The New Exeter Book of Riddles*. Conceived by Lawrence Sail, and initiated by Exeter Phoenix, this anthology consists of one hundred metaphorical riddles (almost all of them specially commissioned) by one hundred English-language poets.

The range of subject matter, form and tone is enormous. The subjects of some – the stars, needle and thread, toe-nails, poetry – would scarcely be out of place in the original Exeter Book, while others – DNA, a supermarket trolley, a mobile 'phone, censorship, the NHS and a getaway car – are unarguably *fin de millénaire*. And as is the case with the first Exeter Book, a few of the new riddles make the most of earthy and witty *double entendres*.

In form, some of these new riddles are close to being conundrums, without being as wilful as Lewis Carroll's 'Why is a raven like a writing desk?', or as unanswerable as W. S. Gilbert's 'Why is a cook's brain like an overwound clock?' At the other end of the spectrum, there are lines that use enigma as a springboard, only to digress and turn into beautiful descriptive poems.

Some of the new riddles echo the non-syllabic, four-stress line of Anglo-Saxon poetry. Some are strictly metrical; some rhyme; some exploit established forms such as the sonnet and villanelle; others are in free verse.

But no matter what the writer's subject, form and tone, the reader is conscious of learning lightly worn, quicksilver imagination, and technical skill. These are necessary ingredients in the making of the metaphorical riddle, and of course they are the outcome of serious endeavour. There is a moving Anglo-Saxon riddle that describes the 'Pen and Three Fingers' (the pen is a quill) advancing across an illuminated manuscript page:

> I watched four curious creatures
> travelling together; their tracks were swart,
> each imprint very black. The birds' support
> moved swiftly; it flew in the air,
> dived under the wave. The toiling warrior
> worked without pause, pointing the paths
> to all four over the beaten gold.

In this anthology, likewise, there are riddles concerned with words and writing: dictionary, pencil, pen, shorthand, computer.

Many riddles appeal both to adults and children. Children, indeed, tend to be more lateral-minded and less literal than their elders, and thus quicker to arrive at solutions. So this adult anthology should also be used widely in schools, by teachers and children alike. Indeed, the National Literacy Strategy makes specific reference to the educational value of riddles.

The New Exeter Book of Riddles extends a form that has always been part of literary tradition. Perhaps more than any other kind of poem, the riddle offers the reader the delight of seeing the familiar as if for the first time. In a late letter to one of the editors, Stephen Spender wrote:

> . . . in *most* poetry which has as subject a concrete or animal thing – Shelley's *Skylark*, say – one begins with the object, the title, the thing, in mind, and then reads the poetry as referring back to this already-conceived idea. The Riddle is back to front. One gets the poetry emanating from the subject – thing – first – and arrives – if one does ever arrive at it – at the title last. The effect is something like pure poetry – a peculiar concentration on imagery – before one arrives at the actual image.

1

I offer you four things
if you will but look:
that which is as great as breath
and greater than food;
the larger part of your cells;
gold from the shadowy depths
(slow-blooded but quicksilver flashing);
and rich thick silt in which
to grow your lotus.

Roselle Angwin

2

The bald head with the fringe
round the neck's nape
straggles in green-grey tongues:
the limp pink stem oozes sap –
my fingers, sticky and black,
thumb each other uncomfortably.

Over the field others crowd,
domed candles under a cathedral sky.

Jane Beeson

3

I live alone where echoes roost,
I tremble like a hill
That is hollow. Capped with stone
To keep me from harm, I tingle
With the bloom of molten breath.

Flown like a kite, I drift
On an easy, ample breeze, letting
The single vowel of time
Enter the world through the door
Of my wholly open mouth.

Charles Bennett

4

I am cuddle-shaped and freckled:
skin me, savour me.

James Berry

5

Black my beginning:
shape of a siren,
talons for fingers.

Round and full after:
still warm to the touch,
safe cupped in my hands.

Full circle my whole:
oil on a puddle
or gleaming shot silk,
myriad colours
imprisoned in glass,
globe floating on air.

Elizabeth Bewick

6

Like the tides I rise and fall.
Like a rock I am unmoved.
Travellers – I take you closer to the stars
but beware lest you stumble.

Patricia Bishop

7

Weird stuff this:
glowing, my head's a wheel of light.

I am tall & strong
need no man to stand behind me, fingering.

She's yeasty with the moon & hurls herself against me
while I give her the glad eye.

Netted in wet skeins, I scream aloud &
white curds spatter.

I'm warning you:
a man could drown in her deceits, her slipperiness.

Elisabeth Bletsoe

8

I chuck their chins,
I've done it through more years
than they are given,
and with so much love.
They stroke me, slide me, glide
and pluck me tenderly,
caress me with a thousand touches.
I lift my voice, my heart, to them,
sing every colour of the gamut,
until the tree that bore me
sighs in every branch,
hums through each leaf,
shrieks in the wind.
Afterwards my songs
run their melodies in the dark.

Anne Born

9

A punt gliding under a chain of smiles

A point in history
the slight sway
the terrifying glimpse
of a ravine

A small wrought iron consideration
One man's design over-arching
Two people considering whether to

Tilla Brading

10

Your fingers fully awake, it
            fetches up far off
Complete and clear. So you wait
        – then aha! An answer!
You extol it . . . (Fix an exact
        maximum use of
A letter in each of the first
        three lines, in order.)

Alan Brownjohn

11

I have no substance and no form
I am surrounded by what you rid me of
and diminished by what you return
until at last I am fulfilled
and vanish from your sight

Nigel Cameron

12

I saw a great building with many storeys piled high,
Where men and women jostled, pressed all together;
They clamoured aloud, for each had a tale to tell:
I listened awhile and I came away wiser.

Tony Charles

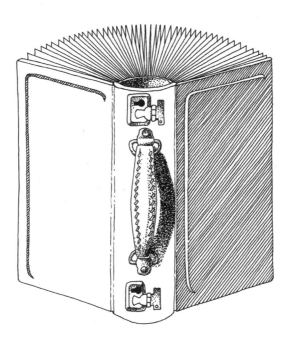

13

All afternoon I hope
it'll come back – rope

of sunlight, silence
of something silk, a sibilance,

the turning pages of a book,
a breath that made me look.

Its soft elision parts the grass
just long enough to pass,

a word unspooled from somewhere,
the fluent freehand signature

of flood, of cool *couleuvre*
in a most un-Roman swerve

of Celtic knotwork, the heart's
blood-beat, the holy art

of gilding in the grass, a glance
of flame, a flamboyance.

Gillian Clarke

14

What we reminded you of you are already forgetting,
You are already imagining something new.
Close your eyes, remember the way we move:
In your sleepless nights we will help you to let go.

David Constantine

15

For being unfaithful though ever true
the rapacious age imprisoned me,
stretched on the rack in concealing shadow
my skin singed as choicest delicacy.

Though faces glimpsed from my window
smile blithely in upon the deed,
I bear their pleasure, assuage their sorrow,
an immortal coil of mortal greed.

Christopher Cook

16

We are a crystal zoo,
Wielders of fortunes,
The top of our professions.
Like hard silver nails
Hammered into the dark
We make charts for mariners.

John Cotton

17

They're marked men. Their park is like an open prison,
all rules and rectangles, semi-circles, mesh
they stake out with grunts and squirts of saliva.
Blows to their heads, whistling in their ears –
they see damned spots, run themselves ragged
before baying hordes or dank, dimming spaces:
blowing, breathless almost, their mouths still stuffed
with efs and cant as they tussle over the moon.

Kevin Crossley-Holland

There is a whole world involved in me.
Open me up and look. Like God, I give rise
to novelties like the *parbuckle*, the bright *pardelote*,
or pain-killing *paregoric*. It smacks of Eden
as you peer through my open gates and learn,
as if a perfect myth, from first to last, has done
what art and science can only dream of –
but beware, think of me as a crutch, or a friend,
as a fall-back for your ignorance only so far:
hard as you might look, you are not mentioned here.

Martyn Crucefix

19

I start with a straight back and two points.
    If pressed my points may flatten against the sheet.
Turn me on the double bed in other joints
    And have me spread my legs in the mating-feat.

Some people take and put me under their thumb
    Because I will not bend to suit their liking.
I may be hard-pressed but they'll succumb,
    If they don't grant me space, to a good spiking.

Many will seek my narrow bed, my slot.

Peter Dale

20

When I lean down to stir the bathwater
are they reaching down into the river
contours – do they know where I am?

When I am silent do they give up
their own silences like hasty barricades?
Do they root in the shine of river

grow thoughtful, shine and renew with me
in childhood, adolescence, middle age –
come to each region of my life with me?

Are theirs the gestures I make – forgetful,
candid, slow? And do their sighs
and open-hearted laughs reach out

into the breeze-ways of every small town
I have ever driven through?

Jane Duran

21

Alive, I flourish
in the seeds of flowers
Crushed, I soothe your skin
and ease your pain

Forced from my grave
to power your tools
I linger as a curse
and foul your air

Essence of life slips from your grasp
Your wealth comes from a rotted corpse

Edna Eglinton

22

My emblem is an arrow
as dangerous as a blade
or bullet. My mark meaningless
or deep, ugly or beautiful.
My sheath often blue or black.
I fit the hand of everyone.

John Fairfax

23

A door
In homes
I have no hole
Those who flash through me
I am way out
For the night-watchers,

but not a door
but not for humans
for a key, nor a handle,
having no fingers.
and way in
the long-whiskered.

U. A. Fanthorpe

24

Without you, I prefer the nights:
the darkness inside me

like the darkness around. All day
I am alone with my emptiness:

a white space, with nothing to feed it
but light and shadow.

My claw feet can't follow you.
I have no voice to call you.

I only know you are near by scents –
orange oil, or lavender – and by a heat

that creeps up my cold skin
and tells me I will feel again

the weight of your body. You have no idea
how wonderful it is to hold you,

to have you lie so still, so happy.
When you move, I hear a whoosh

and you touch me in so many places
I'm trembling and tingling.

It's spoiled by fear of your going.
Sometimes, I pretend I'm a cradle

for you to sleep in – but you always wake;
or a womb – but you still escape,

leaping out and leaving me.
So, next time, I'll be a coffin

filled with chilling water
in which you will stay for ever.

Vicki Feaver

25

Gifted with vision the snowman would see
through what I am. In the heart of winter
I come from my fields to enter
your home in a sack.

Once I wore green; soon, dangerous in red,
my tongues will burn with history: the ponies blind
and blackened men, their livings brought me
here, the villages broken and left for dead.
Later, going out, I'm already out of mind.

Frank Fell

26

Ask many women and they'll claim no knowledge, but some
may tell of being stranded and one in France with a husband
furious that despite her A-level she didn't know the word for it.
If you're female, and asking at the bar, men will look askance
but then give you plenty plenty what you want: blown off the gauge
and steaming. Cork. Warped. Apprentices use itchy laddertape in manways
under pressure, swallowed by blackness that stays in mouths, in skin, in
lungs for days. Strap it, hold it till it gets hard. Boy racers squeeze
a vivid kind of toothpaste. Three men come close to their allowable annual
dose to cut the old away, insert two new, underwater, with the head off.

Jennie Fontana

27

Rarest of the esculents, its distribution
so wayward as to seem almost wilful,
it is sought in a kind of dance
along paths you can never retrace,
every step taken for you, and the woods
closing behind you with every step.
Just when you are lost, when the woods themselves
seem at a loss, it discloses itself,
a hidden fold, flower of the fork.
Chew softly, undressed or with a little yoghurt.

Roger Garfitt

28

I am the difficult silk that slides from your grasp,
I am lace petticoats and the knee-high swirl,
I am an old sea-captain's white moustache,
I am the perm that will not hold its curl,
I am the land's dropped slip and rising shift,
I am a piece of froth, a bagatelle,
I am relinquishment and eternal theft,
I am a gesture of greeting and farewell.

Elizabeth Garrett

You lie with me nightly. In bathrooms I'm there
to dry your wet body and turban your hair.

I cover your table and lie on your knee
and even the table itself may be me.

I'm casement and sash set in every façade.
I'm letterbox, letter and holiday card,

a bill or a book; a box, a desk drawer,
a stair tread, a hearth rug, a floor tile, a door.

I'm a figure symmetrical, rigid and straight,
something man, and not nature, has learned to create.

Pamela Gillilan

30

I flash for megabucks
        expose
glamourbonk neckcrunch limbglitz
            enlarge
broken bored listless lives
                    snap
rich kiss-splattered trysts
shoot
        beauty bleeding
click
        throatgape
                    clickclick
                            thrustguts
clickclickclick

Diana Gittins

31

More powerful than the government,
I make the roads smell sweet.
I fuzz through air, jump the horizon.
I consist of colourless lines, yet

swash surfaces to brightness.
At night I bleed myself into dreams.
Once I am caught, I cease,
although I brim with what I was.

Giles Goodland

32

When my stomach bulges, I hurl wild whoops
of laughter into topsy air, and I wait like water
for something like a splash of limbs. My legs
are short, stubby and hard. I can show you sun,
moon or sky, although you'll rather see yourself
dishevelled, flailing, a wallop of body.
I make you open out, I make you tumble
and windmill and giddy. So tell me my name.

Bill Greenwell

33

Two spiral stairs we climb to bed together.
Each step creaks a different who-goes-there.
Each taps the morse that codes us to each other,
ringing through the walls of cells we share.
The twisted zip ripped open in the fumbling
of life's *yes!* to life. Can this be all it means:
after the quick thrill, the roulette-wheel tumble,
each slips back into the other's crumpled genes?

Philip Gross

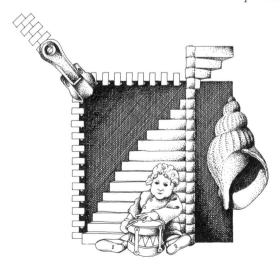

No fragrance yet the fold
translated to pallor
of sulphur on gold draws
back summer dusks freighted
with memory – head bent
in anticipation
of pleasure – albeit
these overlapping flakes
(ivory shadow-furred)
offer the expectant
touch no texture except
a bland slipperiness –
however, seen edge-on,
this instant taken out
of time rules an almost
undetectable white
line in the lighted room
and if turned in the hand
will reveal when reversed
the disquieting fact
there's nothing behind it

Harry Guest

35

My skin shimmers with all the colours
of a rainbow, and you hold me like a feather,
so gently, afraid to smear my shine with
your fingertips, reading me closely, spinning
me in your mind, gently placing me
in the black box where I whirr
contentedly, singing with my silver tongue.

Charles Hadfield

36

Narrow for love that must be fitted in.
Since we can hardly marry, just as wide
As cotton lies between a groom and bride.
So there will be no gap between us, thin.
(My King, your Queen, half empty, out of bounds.)
It looks convincing when the bill arrives –
The space that we can spare from both our lives,
Twelve for a night instead of twenty pounds.
Designed for one and given up by ten
Once made it will (like love) be made again.

Sophie Hannah

37

I work in the evening, alone and in silence
My book's always open all the year round
But when light is poor I put down my brush.
I redeem the blankness, embellish white space,
Press gold onto leaves, gilding the edges.
I crimson the plush of curling roses
And ring with corn-light the crowns of pilgrims.
As darkness approaches I dash off last rubrics
Wash out my brush in reddening water
Sink into bed and snuff out my lantern.

James Harpur

38

The hair on your body,
says the man in the moon,
each night as we boogie –
if we could but embrace
each night as you swoon –
would tickle my face.

David Hart

39

I am a glider on time's thermals,
slowing perception in the amber hours.
I sound no horn, flare no lights,
clarions and fanfares are unnecessary distractions.

Speed is immaterial
though some passengers understood its implications.
My gears all propel at constant velocity;
there is no reverse.

You will all feel my shadow as I pass,
see yourselves in black coachwork
and your arm will gradually lift,
thumb extended to hitch a ride.

John Hawkhead

40

I am the swift scribble,
quicksilver hieroglyphics
accelerated onto a page.
I am a common code,
corporate runes,
the secret way
by which you might say
I love you.

Patricia Hawkhead

I'm skulking by the scandal and the handle
on the door

I'm stuff that you want off the cuff, I'm friendly
with the poor

I'm of a mind where females are defined as bits
of skirt

I'm what you want to keep out when you've got
an open hurt

John Hegley

42

Though starlings imitate me
I'm no rat in feathers
but I spread infection like pigeons.
Unlike my parents I'm migratory
but I'm not caught in mist-nets to be ringed.
Who will I pass my number on to
when I die?

Michael Henry

43

Grab the beast by the horns.
Wrestle it down the narrow streets
till you break its will
to skitter its own way.
Subdue it. Burden its rib-cage.
Let your children ride.
And then let it stray.
Who cares? They'll send
a herdsman to round it up
at the end of the day.

Stuart Henson

44

I do not have a body
yet I grow constantly.

Everyone wants to visit
yet no one wants to live with me.

Nobody can find me
yet in the end,

like the stuff between the stars,
I shall be everywhere.

Bill Herbert

45

Who's that knocking on my ring, says the chin.
Me, says the stranger, I want to come in.

Selima Hill

I can lift gravity's stern glower,
I tickle her armpit with my sleight of hand.
Sample my circus skills: my real rope trick's
to lay my high wire even as I walk it,
and look how far my trapeze flies –
all the way the air's back bears me.

Scared that in spite of all you'll see
gravity turn on me and swat me?
Inspect my safety net – then watch
how soft she lets me light beneath it.
My circus kills, but not this acrobat!
Now if I spin much more you'll guess me quick.

Libby Houston

47

In grandfather's house I ran up and down,
at one time always down. Then to the stars
larger than life, an icon of mischief
with spindly legs. And now I'm in business
cut down to size, a director with only
one ball, but handled with care I perform
exceedingly well – though nothing can match
the comforts of a hole.

Doris Hulme

48

I am a winged creature, flightless,
No legs, yet I carry you away,
I speak with many voices,
Teller of necessary lies.

Su Jarwood

Who could have baked my entire heart's desire
and flung it so high
to float with the stars and the moon?
And how can I reach what I want most
but don't want to eat? Can you name it
and swallow the tall tale I'm talking about?

Sylvia Kantaris

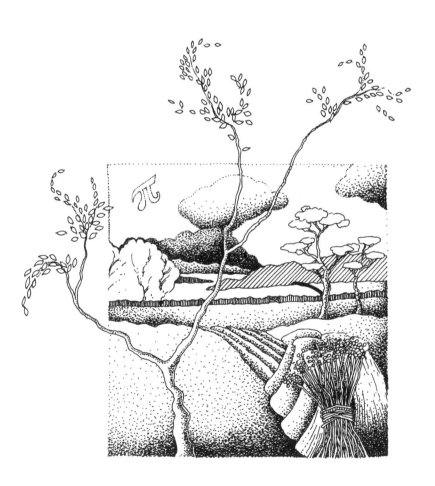

50

One eye crystal, one eye flame, it arrives
by stealth. Carrying tatters in its jaw,
nimbus in its hair. Who can tell on water
if shadow's nibbling into light or light
at shadow's edge? Thus, it is mouth and tail,
hoof and horn, ice or thaw, none knows what rears
its head. It scavenges on breath. Baits ear
and voice, voice and ear, by these it mates.
Eradicates, illuminates. Done, hunches
down to ponder how weak, how bright, its chain.

Mimi Khalvati

51

I am chained,
A solitary prisoner
The colour of fire;
I squat on water
And bob with its breathing
And the wind's temper;
A triangular hat
That won't sink.
On my left
My Janus face
Says: 'Shun me.'
On my right
I give freedom.

Lotte Kramer

52

I'm not in court to be judged,
but I am the mark by which others are.
The bottomless find scant use for me.

Jenny Lewis

53

I quake like Satan
in a burning lake.
At first too hot to take
I'm soon too cold.
I bring hot fingers to sell,
a tang of sea, I fill
a street with my smell
and pile a plate with gold.

Herbert Lomas

54

I flourish between pleasure and pain.
Lovers make love during my season.
One of my names says breezy branches,
Another a young man's downy chin.
The third remains a thorny problem.
Farmers stamp on my feet for fodder.
Now I'm a chimney sweep, now a broom.

Michael Longley

55

Not like a sock. The one
lost, the same as the one
still here. Matching. A pair.
Nor like an aim or a moral
you can no longer afford.
More like someone you had
slipping away from you.

Not like a memory you search
every drawer for. Nor like
the argument with the law
when words failed you.
More like the self
you had before the parade
and the one she had and lost
and looks for in water.

Mary Maher

If you're looking for water
I can point out the way.
I am a running river,
I'm covered by hay.

You use me to ask questions
and listen well to this,
since I'm the penultimate Roman
you must precede me with a kiss!

Tinker Mather

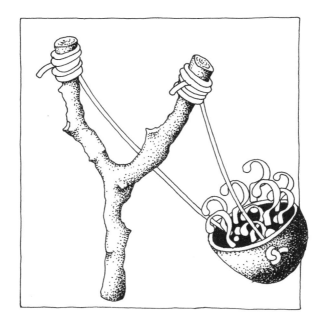

57

A slow train. Few travellers. If
we were real we'd be out of service.

No one gets on or off. We speak
softly, as does the man in charge

whispering intercessions
like the hiss of escaping steam.

Under the arched roof, our smoking breath –
the creak of a cough at the fourteenth stop

and the end of the line.

Eleanor Maxted

58

Though giving pleasure to many
I am no more than a passing fancy,

A bagatelle. Am looked down upon
by my peers for my sense of fun.

Jealous introverts, they think me flippant.
Silver-tongued I may be, but not irreverent.

I glister, am all show, all style.
Here is the key, come inside: I'll make you smile.

Roger McGough

59

I wear bright colours
And bow, gracefully, to the ground
But I'm fading away, fading away

Elma Mitchell

60

Twilight by the plantation.
I heard the hope of summer come alive to his chime.
Then a can was dropped in the dairy.
The sheep began to bleat.
In the faraway farm, the door slammed –
The light put out in the porch.
Sound of a bat, a may-bug,
The motorbike into the next parish.
By the plantation, the second chime –
Summer's hope torn in two.

John Moat

Mine is the ungloved
pulsing fingertip,

the shroud, the interlace
of brittle leaves.

I am the sculpture of your stiffened
hosepipe's tangle

and a light-scored requiem,
a glittering stave.

Mine is the cruel purity
that snaps all iron,

sends your warm breath
biting backwards.

I am the splintered rainbow
locked in ice,

the broken promise
of an early spring.

John Mole

What can I tell you? Though your quarry
lies exhausted at the bottom of an exhausted quarry,

to follow that lure
will almost certainly end in failure.

While I did indeed sink
like a stone among bottles, cans, a fridge, a sink,

a slab of marble, granite
or slate I'm not. By the window of an All-Nite

Café or a 24-Hour Bank
I, too, stretched as if on a flowery bank

and admired
my shiny, former self, a self even then mired

in the idea that what you saw
was what you got.

Why would a hostage's hand hacked off with a hacksaw
weigh on me now like a blood-spattered ingot

from that 24-Hour Bank, I who once cut such a figure
in its drive-up window? Go figure.

Paul Muldoon

63

The tall Wood twins
grip each other everywhere:
'It's all right, we're only
standing in for Lady Stair.'

Les Murray

64

Not loved enough, nor yet quite lost,
No longer fought for, nor yet forgot,
My well being, once rightfully yours
(Of no account in your accounting),
Is set aside to count the cost.
So then, farewell:
I am too dear for your possessing.

Suniti Namjoshi

65

Men stare at me more than at women
these days. But what matter –
I click with them too! In the days
when Socrates was the bees' knees
I was speaking stone, but the jaws
really hurt so I ended up talking riddles –
but at least I'd invented that genre!
Now, though, folks, I'm back
cleverer than ever, and so full of answers
you'll not get rid of me again.

William Oxley

Through frost and snow and sunlight,
through rain and night and day
I go back to where I come from.
I pass all things, yet stay.

Brian Patten

67

I am first mouth, then hand,
aired together for a message
that always means the same.
I am sent as the crow would go,
but although some pretend to catch me,
my fate is to fly forever,
never to arrive.

Edwyna Prior

68

I hang from a thin green rope
and sway in the wind and rain.
I guard my treasure in a wooden safe
which no one can steal
unless they first beat me to death.

Elizabeth Rapp

Soon and silently,   in a dark suit . . .
men at the mead-bench,   meditate, name him.

Peter Reading

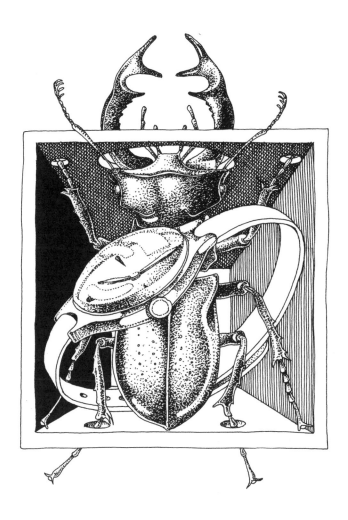

70

Your job's to work the surface. Don't
go too deep.

A spit's just fine. Leave
the unconscious mind alone

though you may bless
the commas that wriggle and slither up.

You make it go from left to right:
lines of scrawl along

and down a page.
The story follows on

and on. The plot's
rich metaphor. You keep on

turning it over
and over.

Michèle Roberts

71

You need me for sitting
Though I'm not a chair.
When you're running
I'm still there.
People say I'm soft
But I'm hard to find
'Cos wherever you look
I'm always behind.

Michael Rosen

72

Like cancer cells, ivy, arthritis,
Lips on a window, a lie,
A waistline, a stain you keep rubbing,
The spaces hands make to deny:
Like fire and the rumour of fire,
Its nature is always to spread.
It will blossom in public and private,
And loves to take root in your head.

Carol Rumens

73

Up and down I go, my stock
rising and falling. I hang on
by the merest fluke. Thanks to me
calmly the bare masthead nods,
riding under the bright stars.

Lawrence Sail

74

Men rigged my chamfered oak
and fed me glass, commanded
the ghostly world stand still.
Now my nose is into weather,
executions, nudes – dumb horror
speaks to my one vocable.
I imitate the painters, stiffen limbs.
Smiles come at me like refugees.

William Scammell

75

Although you never asked to come with me,
without you, there'd have been no staring down
on Alps in crumpled silk, a scratchcard sea,
the silent converse of a sunstruck town
which slid its web beneath our flying perch.
I pat you absent-mindedly to prove
you didn't up and leave me in the lurch
and turbulence of all this on-the-move.
Stick close, my bur; now please these colder eyes
alert for glitches, some hiatus where
the truth between us lies – and if it lies
could leave things, as we were, up in the air.
  Let country customs take their time, renew
  time spent, mis-spent, each time I glance at you.

Peter Scupham

76

Together, babe, we could have had the world sewn up.
You filled my eye, I kept you in stitches. When we moved together
we glided – no hitches. Yes, sometimes I needled you. Too pushy,
you claimed. But you – so spineless, so easy, you always needed me
to drag you through. Yet, life's so unfair. For I'm the one left empty,
threadbare. While you, Mr Sleazy, without me to keep you
on the straight and narrow, you still manage to thread your way, tying
everything – as you did me – up in knots.

Olive Senior

I am always behind
or on top of you.
Full of dust, ash and air,
I smell of every room
you ever walked through.
I rise when offended,
creak when wet. How
easily we part, adieu,
how often I leave trails
of myself in your wake.

Jo Shapcott

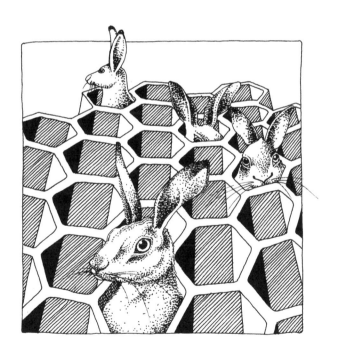

78

Many creatures don't have one.
But I have two.
Each one is a loner, but lives with four brothers.
How well in a cradle this creature soothes.

Penelope Shuttle

79

It's night, an extra quilt,
making love's a treat.
Concessions, catch the second bus,
a lady offers up her seat.

People mumble, print is small,
the light is poor. A gin imparts
a half a kick; no wine
to oil the rusty gate.

Most lines are kind.
Lost things are slow to find.
Expect a moss to germinate,
little else to grow. Tell them:
sell fast-forward pills.

Steve Sims

80

I have a voice in my head that talks backwards.
So if I walk backwards I can hear it properly
But I haven't got eyes in the back of my head
So I walk forwards and listen to it backwards instead.

Lemn Sissay

81

Conjure with me: three letters
Of the alphabet, or two and one, or one.
Run me backwards and I would seem to be unchanged,
But that would be an uphill task of course.
My name speaks of former times,
While I am still current;
Though what current can be still?

Richard Skinner

82

Rumoured thief,
cursed singular:
a ratchet rattle
picker of ideas.

Sam Smith

83

Time and again we're cut down to size,
Long out of favour and too low-borne.
In our extended family, however, well-placed close cousins
Brighten dull display – not too loud, not too flash.
Jealous of all the attention, we feel undermined.
But we don't stay turned in on ourselves. Growing
in confidence,
We make a stand for unrestricted life,
Until once more we're cut down to size.

Martin Sorrell

84

Man.
Fish.
First fruit.

Unicorn.
Pelican.
Second of Three.

Word Man.
Hanged Man.

Christopher Southgate

85

I am black-browed,
a maverick in the white nights,
my eye keen as obsidian,
my field mischievous as glass.
I am so close to the surface
I shape the sun on the drowning.
When drift-nets foul the propellers
hang me round your neck.

Pauline Stainer

86

Something you won't ever bring pressure to bear on;
    wafer on the tongue, sip of wine,
a symbol of nourishment, itself a symbol
    of what can't be consumed or felt.
    You might wish to say it is like
    the way the wind seems to blow light
on cloudy days across the surface of the sea.
    You'd be utterly mistaken.

Every Christmas my daughter speaks Old Slavonic
    over mushroom and cabbage soup,
    over portions of river carp.
    I hear, but barely understand.
  I barely understand: a true comparison.

James Sutherland-Smith

87

I pull opposites together.
I'm more use than ornament.
If it were not for me
Some virgin's modesty
Might very well collapse.
The gallant Scots will clasp me.
I ride upon their laps.
I mean no harm though my cold steel
Might run them through perhaps.

Guida Swan

Even now I cannot help thinking of them
as historical. The noise they make drowns
out the radio static of the street. Grey gowns
of rain flutter or run away in a million gem
spectacular but these dark suns expand
and guard us from the present danger which
is simply a drench of brilliants, rich
as the flood. Look, children, I hold out my hand
beyond its perimeter fence. The fine
spray gathers in my palm then dies away.
I close the black sun and hobble off with it.
It sighs as it closes, approximates to a line
or a stick, like the day before yesterday,
or the meetings of a wartime cabinet.

George Szirtes

I'm ugly but I don't know why
my friends aren't actually my friends.
I knot your gut and make you cry.

Part of me is good. I try
to tell you. Look how your arm bends.
I'm ugly but I don't know why.

It happens when my mouth goes dry.
A kind of greenish cloud descends.
I knot your gut and make you cry.

Don't say you like me. It's a lie.
I know how everyone pretends.
I'm ugly but I don't know why.

I home in on your weakness. I
might use it. Or not. It depends.
I knot your gut and make you cry.

I ridicule and terrify.
These are the means that serve my ends.
I'm ugly, but I don't know why
I knot your gut and make you cry.

Sandra Tappenden

90

I am true in the land of ancient sounds
where words and thoughts are stones unmarked.
I flee from riddles that spew from your lips
and the paper and metal that pass from hand to hand;
rattling mouths stamped on meaningless faces.
My eyes are of the wood where you hunt deer and foxes;
fear is a substance as solid as earth.
You invent mean faces for me, squint and as ugly as sin
and a story which reaches beyond my ken,
your beautiful baby carried away.

Susan Taylor

91

The radial wheels of the season spiked with knives:
The hand which investigates such workmanship
Needs to go gauntleted, or leave it to the eyes:
Boudicca's bladed chariots rode like these,
Flesh flinching from them through the laid-waste field
That autumn has now invaded with this crop.

Charles Tomlinson

92

Then suddenly his brain became the sound
and shape and nerve of breathless requiems,
of songs in which there glowed all warmth and light,
all colour, touch and wisdom that the earth
could give. His eyes swung upon the poles
of many globes. He felt the returning tide
through time and space come throbbing through the tips
of all his fingers, flooding his dry veins
with rich green sap, giving him new sight
to every sense, making him whole again.

Raymond Tong

93

In cities I'm as rare as I'm unwelcome,
banished from the gaps between the stars,
confined to filing cabinet and basement,
glove compartment, wardrobe, luggage, lung.
But open all these traps and you won't free me.

You turn the light out but the curtains glow.
Shut your eyes and still you don't see *me*
but shimmerings of multi-coloured mist.
You're getting warmer, though. If you could swivel
your inner eye you'd find me close behind you.

James Turner

94

I have horns, but am not beast,
though some would suck my flesh
drawn forth on spears

I walk the world on my stomach,
backwards down lanes of nails,
never leaving my house

follow my trail slowly –
my mould will still be unbroken
when I am gone

Gordon Wardman

95

I paid a spring-time visit to your county.
Primrose and violet starred the lanes, lambs waved catkin tails
and the red earth glowed in cheery welcome. Long expected,
I was a punctual guest, dazzling you with my mirrored glory.
Like the old lanthorn of our last encounter I lit the darkest moor
and field, exchanged a passing nod with owl and badger,
greeted the first of summer birds returning to your shores,
as I shall do again one day.

Jean West

96

the big sleep, the high window,
the little sister, the long goodbye.

the long awakening, the wee small door,
the high sister, the big hallo.

the long sleep, the long window,
the long sister, the short goodbye.

the sleeping sister, the long littleness,
the windowed brevity, the brief adieu.

the soaring casement,
the colossal slumber,
the female sibling of less-than-average stature,
the unattenuated leavetaking

(farewell my lovely lady in the lake)

playback

John Whitworth

97

The inscrutable question,
the singular question,
the question with a quest in its tail.
'What does it all mean?' I ask you,
set on the lines or read between.
What walks with three legs
in the evening,
why is a raven like a writing-desk
and what have I got in my pockets?

Simon Williams

Everything opaque about us, perhaps
that's why they fill us with holes
and hang our heads for trophies –
to cut us down to size.

Down: where our number is heading
and what you can't get from us –
us with our ironing-board skin,
ears like the maps of continents,

the car-tyre screech of our cries.

Anthony Wilson

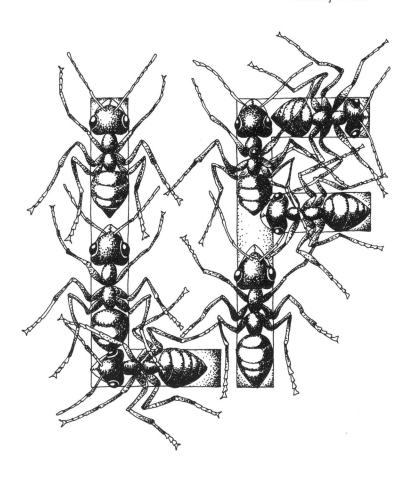

99

I go through the wood in silence
and come out on to the snow
where I leave my prints
though I have no footsteps,
where I speak your heart
though I cannot breathe.

Kit Wright

100

I love your plumpness.
Ripe, brown skin
puckered like a camel's nose.
I want to squeeze you end to end,
roll the promise of you
between my teeth
till your rum soul whistles
and sun floods me.

Sally Young

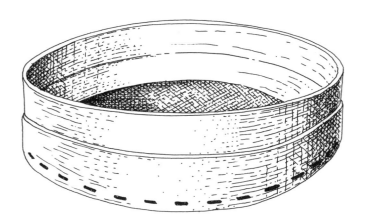

Answers

1 Pond
2 Dandelion clock
3 Bell
4 Ripe banana
5 Witch-ball
6 Flight of stairs
7 Automatic lighthouse
8 Violin
9 Bridge
10 Fax
11 Hole in the ground
12 Bookcase
13 Grass snake
14 Clouds
15 Roll of film
16 Stars
17 Footballers
18 Dictionary
19 Staple
20 Ancestors
21 Oil
22 Parker pen
23 Cat-flap
24 Bath
25 Coal
26 Gasket
27 Oyster mushroom
28 Wave
29 Rectangles
30 Paparazzo
31 Rain
32 Trampoline
33 DNA
34 Black and white photograph
35 Compact disc
36 Single bed in a hotel room
37 Sunset
38 Grass
39 Hearse
40 Shorthand
41 Dirt
42 Mobile 'phone
43 Supermarket trolley
44 The past
45 Door-knocker
46 Spider
47 Mouse
48 Theatre
49 Pie in the sky
50 Poetry
51 Buoy
52 Bench
53 Fish and chips
54 Gorse, whin, furze
55 Identity
56 Y
57 Stations of the cross
58 Riddle
59 Rainbow
60 Cuckoo
61 Frost
62 Getaway car
63 Ladder
64 National health service
65 Computer
66 Road
67 Blown kiss
68 Hazelnut
69 Death
70 Digging the vegetable garden
71 Bum
72 Censorship
73 Anchor
74 Camera
75 Passport
76 Needle and thread
77 My hair
78 Thumb
79 Ageing
80 Back words
81 The river Exe
82 Magpie